Building

Altars

Becoming a Living Sacrifice

Dr. David Chapman

**Building Altars:
Becoming a Living Sacrifice**

Dr. David Chapman

Printed in the United States of America. All rights reserved under International Copyright Law. Contents and/or cover may not be reproduced in whole or in part in any form without the expressed written consent of the Publisher.

All Bible quotations are from the New King James Version unless otherwise noted.

Copyright © 2020

**TRU Publishing
1726 S. 1st Ave.
Safford, Arizona 85546**

Table of Contents

Chapter 1: Altars in the Bible 7

Chapter 2: Altar Builders – Part 1, The Patriarchs.......16

Chapter 3: Altar Builders – Part 2, Prophets, Judges & Kings 36

Chapter 4: Memorials 61

Chapter 5: Old Testament Sacrifices 72

Chapter 6: The Believer's Altar....................................84

Dedication

I'd like to dedicate this book on building altars to Jerry Williams of Houston, Texas. Pastor Jerry has been in the ministry for over 50 years. I first knew of him many years ago through his music with his band Harvest. Jerry traveled all over the world and recorded many hits in Contemporary Christian Music. Tens of thousands have come to know Jesus through his ministry. I first met Jerry in 2014 when I invited him to my church to preach and play music. The Lord put an immediate bond between us. Brother Jerry is a close friend, a mentor and an inspiration to me. He is the perfect example of a living sacrifice to the Lord.

Introduction

For many years I have been intrigued by the examples of building altars in the Bible. Whenever I would search to find a resource on the subject, I would invariably come up empty. So I began compiling my own notes and decided to turn it into this small book.

In each occasion where an altar was built, God did something special in the life of the altar builder. Today we no longer build altars made with stones, but rather spiritual altars where we have encounters with the living God.

In this book we will examine each example in the Bible where an altar was built. We will look at the reason it was built as well as the spiritual application.

Chapter 1: Altars in the Bible

Altars

Altars played a significant part in the Old Testament. There are over 400 references to altars in the Bible. Altars were often built to commemorate a divine manifestation such as a Theophany or Christophany that took place at a certain location. A Theophany is a manifestation of God in the Bible that is perceptible and visible to the human senses. A Christophany is a manifestation of the pre-incarnate Christ during the Old Testament period.

Theophany	A manifestation of God in the Bible that is perceptible and visible to the human senses.
Christophany	A manifestation of the pre-incarnate Christ during the Old Testament period.

The patriarchs and prophets of the Old Testament built these altars to memorialize a sacred encounter with the living God. These altars usually included a sacrifice, but sometimes were built simply as a memorial.

In modern times – under the New Covenant, altars have a metaphoric meaning. We don't build literal altars of wood and stone and we certainly don't offer animal sacrifices. Jesus is the perfect Lamb of God and no other blood sacrifice is ever needed for reconciliation to God. But that doesn't mean that altars in the Bible have nothing more than historical significance. When we use the word altar, it can refer to a place where we meet with God and consecrate ourselves to Him. In my local church, I call the front area near the stage an altar area because it's where I invite people to come for prayer.

In this small book we will examine both the historical context – the reason for building each altar, and the spiritual application for us today.

Precise Instructions

The Lord God was very explicit about the building of altars when the Israelites came out of Egypt. In fact, immediately after giving the Ten Commandments, God gave precise instructions on how and why to build altars unto Him.

> **Exodus 20:24-26**
> **24 An altar of earth you shall make for Me, and you shall sacrifice on it your burnt offerings and your peace offerings, your sheep and your oxen. In every place where I record My name I will come to you, and I will bless you.**
> **25 And if you make Me an altar of stone, you shall not build it of hewn stone; for if you use your tool on it, you have profaned it.**
> **26 Nor shall you go up by steps to My altar, that your nakedness may not be exposed on it.**

There are places in our lives that God wants to "record His name." These are the places where God puts His blessing on us. These are sacred times in the life of the believer – times when God reveals Himself and shows His love. The time and place you got saved might be one of those places. For me, I had a very specific encounter with God on a street corner. My life was forever changed from that encounter. There was nothing special about the place; it's just where God chose to record His name indelibly in my heart. I can think of more than a dozen other occasions when I had encounters with God in a life altering way. In most of the encounters I chose to remember them by memorializing them in writing.

A different example of a spiritual altar in my life is a section of Scripture – Psalm 119. Early in my Christian walk I was led by the Spirit to pray through the psalm – all 176 verses, every night. It would take me about an hour and I did this every night for about a year. God met with me every night on that psalm. These many years later I retain the memories of those encounters. When I read Psalm 119 today, it speaks to me in a deeply personal way. That psalm is all about the Word of God and seeking God for understanding of truth. The Lord began to open up incredible revelation out of His Word through those prayers and encounters. Most of everything I know about the Word today, I credit that period of time and those prayers.

Altars were a place of *approach* to Yahweh.

The Lord wants us to draw near to Him. In Old Testament times this often including building an altar as an act of devotion and consecration to God. We still approach God through consecration, but animal sacrifices are not needed, as the blood of the perfect and spotless Lamb of God has been applied to the mercy seat in heaven and we may now enter the throne room of God with boldness.

Hebrews 4: 16 Let us therefore come boldly to the throne of grace, that we may obtain mercy and find grace to help in time of need.

Altars were a place of *worship* of Yahweh.

Altars, foremost, were symbols of worship to Yahweh. God is saying in Exodus 20:24 that He will meet with the worshipper and bless him at the place of the altar. There is nothing physically special about a church building or any of the flooring or furniture inside. But it's a place where people consecrate their hearts and lives to Jesus, so this makes it special. The timing is also important. We need to lay hold of God when the anointing is present. Sometimes people wait until after the church service is over and prayer time has concluded. They will then stop by the pastor's office or catch him in the parking lot and ask for prayer. Prayer works everywhere, but when the anointing of His presence is strong, that's the time to receive a touch from God.

In an atmosphere of worship, we invite the presence of God and He manifests His presence.

2 Corinthians 3:17-18

17 Now the Lord is the Spirit; and where the Spirit of the Lord is, there is liberty.

18 But we all, with unveiled face, beholding as in a mirror the glory of the Lord, are being transformed into the same image from glory to glory, just as by the Spirit of the Lord.

Altars were built with stones without the assistance of tools.

This is a very important instruction. God did not want stones used for the altar that had been shaped with the assistance of human tools. Man is capable of building many things. God gives the gift of craftsmanship to certain people. But in the case of altars, man was not allowed to change the shape of the stones.

Worship must be on God's terms. It's not a matter of building God a wonderful masterpiece of my doing. The altar had to be built with stones that God created and formed without any alteration. Today in the church, we cannot decide for ourselves what will please God. He has said that we must worship Him in Spirit and in truth (John 4:24). All that is born of the flesh is flesh (John 3:6).

As we study through the Bible to understand building altars, the conclusion of the study is that the altar of our heart is where God wants our devotion to be found. This was also true of the patriarchs and prophets who built altars during Bible times. Even though they built physical altars, the Lord was still looking on the heart to find pure devotion to Him. An altar is merely a place where a person consecrates himself in his heart to God.

Indeed, each of us are the temple of God and the Spirit of God dwells within us.

> **1 Corinthians 3:16 Do you not know that you are the temple of God and that the Spirit of God dwells in you?**

During Israel's rebellion and apostasy, the altars of the Lord had been torn down. Elijah, the prophet of God, was called by God to repair the altar of the Lord (1 Kings 18). We will look at this occasion in the Altar Builders chapter. Here in America, this is a time of rebellion and apostasy. Many churches and denominations are turning their backs on the truth of God's Word. The ways of the world are being embraced and the gospel is being watered down. God needs some men and women of God who will repair the altar of the Lord through prayer and consecration.

As you read this book, ask God to put a fire inside your spirit to be fully devoted to God. The Lord will hear those who sincerely call upon Him. I believe that God has a remnant in the land that will passionately follow Him.

"Lord, make me a living sacrifice."

Chapter 1 Review

1. What were altars built to commemorate?

_____

_____

_____

2. What is a way that we might use the word altar in the church today?

_____

_____

_____

3. Altars were a place of _____ to Yahweh and a place of _____ of Yahweh.

4. Why was it important to build the altars without the assistance of tools?

_____

_____

_____

_____

_____

Chapter 2: Altar Builders – Part 1, The Patriarchs

In this section we will examine the various men of God who built altars unto the Lord. We will look at the reason for building the altar and the spiritual application for the believer today.

Noah

> **Genesis 8:20-21**
> **20 Then Noah built an altar to the Lord, and took of every clean animal and of every clean bird, and offered burnt offerings on the altar.**
> **21 And the Lord smelled a soothing aroma. Then the Lord said in His heart, "I will never again curse the ground for man's sake, although the imagination of man's heart is evil from his youth; nor will I again destroy every living thing as I have done.**

Reason for Building the Altar

This is the first altar listed in Scripture. Upon leaving the ark, Noah built an altar and made offerings from every clean animal and every clean bird. God was pleased with the sweet aroma and promised to never again destroy every living thing.

It is not the heart of God to judge and destroy. The Bible says that *God is love* (1 John 4:8). However, God is also holy and as such there must be retribution when *sin's cup* reaches the top and begins to overflow. It should be remembered that God is always calling man to repentance while the cup is not yet full. The Father is longsuffering.

The Lord did concede that man's heart would continue to be dominated by evil (v. 21). This was the case up until the Cross of Christ. Only the blood of Jesus can wash away our sins.

Spiritual Application

God's covenant with Noah represented new beginnings. The altar memorialized God's promise to mankind to never again destroy the earth with a flood. Memorializing encounters with God is a great way to remember all that God does for you. Remembering is even part of the Ten Commandments: *Remember the Sabbath day, to keep it holy* (Exodus 20:8).

We are able to remember that God will never again destroy the earth through a flood because of the sign of the rainbow (Genesis 9:11). God still uses signs and confirmations today. Particular things draw us back to a specific promise that God made.

The believer should erect a spiritual altar of worship and consecration to the Lord whenever God extends a new promise. There will always be a *standing* time before the fulfillment of the promise and finding a way to memorialize the promise will help remind you to trust in God's faithfulness.

Abraham #1

> **Genesis 12:7**
> **Then the Lord appeared to Abram and said, "To your descendants I will give this land." And there he built an altar to the Lord, who had appeared to him.**

Reason for Building the Altar

Upon obeying God to get out from his homeland and go to the land of Canaan, Abraham built an altar when the Lord appeared to him in Canaan. Though he was a stranger in this new country, Abraham kept himself and his family centered on God. There was much to be overwhelmed by, but instead this patriarch built an altar to Yahweh to keep himself grounded and centered.

The Lord appeared unto Abraham in this strange and foreign land. He reaffirmed His promise to Abraham that his seed would possess that land. God always knows what we need and when we need it. I'm sure that Abraham needed this visitation as assurance that he was moving in the right direction.

Spiritual Application

The key to spiritual progress is obedience. Abraham obeyed, not knowing where he was going (Hebrews 11:8). As you step out in obedience to the call of God on your life, you must remember to keep *relationship* to God first. It's easy to get caught up in the new venture and the work that needs to be done, but all true works of God flow out of a life that is yielded to Him.

God appeared to Abraham in Canaan to reaffirm His promise. There are times when we need confirmation *after* we have obeyed the call. We need to hear from

God in our new place, after leaving our comfort zones. Receiving confirmation from God was such a blessing to Abraham that he immediately built an altar of worship unto the Lord.

Don't forget to give God praise throughout each step of your journey. Find a way to memorialize those moments when God speaks to your heart and confirms His promise over you. Writing things down in a journal is always a good way to keep focused on the Lord's instructions.

Abraham #2

> **Genesis 12:8**
> **And he moved from there to the mountain east of Bethel, and he pitched his tent with Bethel on the west and Ai on the east; there he built an altar to the LORD and called on the name of the LORD.**

Reason for Building the Altar

Once more, Abraham built an altar to the Lord in this new and strange land. Abraham pitched his tent east of Bethel and built an altar to the Lord and called on the name of the Lord – Yahweh. As far as Abraham was concerned, wherever he had a tent, God had an altar. What a beautiful picture.

It's important to note that Abraham also returned to the altar after coming up out of Egypt in Genesis 13:1-4, and called on the name of the Yahweh.

Spiritual Application

This altar reminds us of the importance of worship. Abraham called on the name of the Lord – Yahweh. As for Abraham, this meant not only him, but also his whole family. Devotion time as a family is very important in order to keep our lives on track in God's plan.

Do you have an altar of devotion to the Lord in your home? "The family that prays together stays together" is more than a cliché. Families are always on the top of Satan's list of targets. Make sure that there is an altar with your tent.

When Abraham came up out of Egypt he remembered the altar and returned to call on the name of the Lord again. Once more, this emphasizes the great importance on remembering your encounters with God. This suggests that we should not move on from our altars too soon. We should come back to the encounters we have with God time and again. Romans 11:29 tells us that the gifts and calling of God are irrevocable. For that reason, we should abide in our calling. This means times of reflecting and allowing the Holy Spirit to echo into our lives God's purpose. This keeps us refreshed.

Abraham #3

> **Genesis 13:18**
> **Then Abram moved his tent, and went and dwelt by the terebinth trees of Mamre, which are in Hebron, and built an altar there to the Lord.**

Reason for Building the Altar

Upon the promise from God of giving Abraham the land, Abraham walked through it and pitched his tent by the terebinth trees of Mamre in Hebron and built an altar there to the Lord.

Prior to this encounter, Abraham and Lot, his nephew, parted ways. Lot and his party went to the Jordan Valley and Abraham settled in the land of Canaan (Genesis 13:10-12). Here again, we see Abraham demonstrating the need to keep the Lord in the center of his activities. Abraham was displaying the character trait of consistency during this time period. This is something that would pay dividends later.

Spiritual Application

We should always express gratefulness to God for His great promises. Even when the plan changes, such as Lot and Abraham separating, God remains faithful. The Lord knows all of the things that will happen along the way before they ever occur. His promises stand firm regardless of the situation or the changes that may occur.

Others may wonder why you stay faithful and always put God first. There may even be times when you wonder why you're doing it.

Keep building altars of devotion to God. Maintain a consistent worship life. Always take time to reflect and remember your encounters with God. This builds a spiritual history with the Lord and prepares you for greater things in the future.

Abraham #4

> **Genesis 22:9**
> **Then they came to the place of which God had told him. And Abraham built an altar there**

and placed the wood in order; and he bound Isaac his son and laid him on the altar, upon the wood.

Reason for Building the Altar

There is much to consider when reading the story of Abraham offering his only son, Isaac, in obedience to God. The entire story is found in Genesis chapter 22 beginning in verse one through verse 19. Clearly, as the text reads (v 1), God was testing Abraham. He was told to offer his only son Isaac as a burnt offering (v 2). This is the second occurrence of a burnt offering in the Bible – Noah's being the first (Genesis 8).

Abraham's faith was so strong that he believed God would raise his son from the dead (Hebrews 11:19). Abraham told his servants, "Stay here with the donkey; the lad and I will go yonder and worship, and we will come back to you." Notice that Abraham said *we*, not I will come back to you.

As they traveled forward to their destination of Moriah, young Isaac questioned his father about the nature of the offering (Genesis 22:7-8).

Genesis 22:7-8

7 Then he [Isaac] said, "Look, the fire and the wood, but where is the lamb for a burnt offering?"

8 And Abraham said, "My son, God will provide for Himself the lamb for a burnt offering."

Abraham knew that God would provide. The whole scenario was a typology of the cross. Jesus, the Lamb of God would provide Himself as the offering for the sins of the world.

Abraham obeyed, considering the act as one of worship to Yahweh. God stopped Abraham as he raised the knife, telling him "Now I know that you fear the Lord" (v 12).

The Lord already *knew* the outcome through His omniscience (all-knowing), but now He knew through covenant relationship with His servant and friend Abraham.

God provided a ram in Isaacs's place (v 13). The burnt offering was made to the Lord and God revealed Himself that day as Yahweh-Yireh (aka Jehovah-Jireh), which means, "The Lord will provide" (v 14).

Spiritual Application

Every child of God will go through the test of obedience. The Lord never places His children in a situation and requires obedience where and when the demand is too great. We must learn that all tests from God are designed to promote us, not to fail us. Abraham would have never progressed beyond the father of Isaac to the father of nations without passing this test. There are things that God wants to do in each of our lives that can only be accomplished by passing the test of obedience.

In Biblical interpretation, there is a rule called *the law of first mention*. This means that the first time a word or subject is mentioned in the Bible, it carries additional weight in how the subject should be understood. The word worship (v 5) is introduced in our English Bibles in this story. Often we think of worship as merely singing a song or lifting our hands. To Abraham, worship meant the sacrifice of all that was most valuable to him. It meant holding nothing back from God. Our worship should not be viewed as any less. Though God will not ask us to place our child on an altar as a sacrifice, He will require of us all that we cherish, if it becomes an idol in our lives.

Ultimately, because Abraham passed the obedience test, God revealed Himself as Yahweh-Yireh, "the Lord will provide." When God asks for a step of faith, He will reward with His provision.

Of course, the greatest message in this story are the words, "God will provide for Himself the lamb" (v 8). This statement foretold the cross. Jesus was the Lamb of God slain from the foundations of the world (Revelation 13:8).

Isaac

> **Genesis 26:25**
> **So he built an altar there and called on the name of the Lord, and he pitched his tent there; and there Isaac's servants dug a well.**

Reason for Building the Altar

The Lord appeared to Isaac and told him not to fear but that He would bless and multiply his descendants for His servant Abraham's sake (v 24). Isaac was greatly blessed by the Lord. When he planted his crops that year, he harvested a hundred times more grain than he planted (v 12). But all of the prosperity made the Philistines very jealous. He had to go through persecution and hardships. But in the end, God reiterated the promise He'd made to Abraham, his father.

The Philistines had filled up Isaac's wells with dirt – wells that had been dug in Abraham's time. When he dug a new well in the Gerar Valley, the local shepherds claimed that the water was theirs. Isaac let it go and moved on. He was finally able to have enough land to prosper, so he dug another well. After another move to Beersheba, the Lord appeared to him to reiterate His promise that He'd made to Abraham. Isaac built and altar and dug yet another well.

Spiritual Application

God will prosper you even in the most adverse circumstances. The Lord gave Isaac an increase that was a hundredfold. Which, incredibly, is what Jesus promised in the gospel of Mark.

> **Mark 10:29-30**
> **29 So Jesus answered and said, "Assuredly, I say to you, there is no one who has left house or brothers or sisters or father or mother or wife or children or lands, for My sake and the gospel's,**
> **30 who shall not receive a hundredfold now in this time—houses and brothers and sisters**

and mothers and children and lands, with persecutions—and in the age to come, eternal life.

Jesus promised a hundredfold *with* persecutions. Persecution can happen in different ways. Sometimes, as was the case with Isaac, you have to be willing to move on. Sometimes we are holding tightly to the things the Lord wants us to hold loosely.

God keeps His promises and building altars is a great way to remind yourself that He hasn't forgotten. Two important things that God remembers and forgets, respectively: He remembers His promises (Psalm 105:8) and He forgets our sins (Hebrews 10:17). Because of this, we are able to start anew with God's grace.

When your well dries up, find out where God wants you and dig another well. But don't forget to build an altar and keep God first in all that you do.

Jacob #1

Genesis 33:20
Then he erected an altar there and called it El Elohe Israel.

Reason for Building the Altar

Jacob had wrestled with God (chapter 32) and reconciled with Esau (33:1-17). He then came into Canaan and erected an altar and called it El Elohe Israel – God, the God of Israel (v 20).

This was near the first altar that Abraham had built about 185 years earlier (Genesis 12:7). Jacob learned from his father Isaac that where they pitch a tent, they build an altar. What a great lesson to teach your children. He named the altar "The God of Israel is God" (NET Bible). Jacob was Israel. His relationship was personal and not just his fathers' religion.

Jacob was giving thanks to the Lord for his safe return to the land of his fathers. He also built the altar as a way of taking possession of the place.

Spiritual Application

Our relationship with God, though influenced by others, needs to be personal and intimate. Jacob (Israel) said, "The God of Israel is God." My God is the God of the universe! Having personal encounters with God helps to establish a deep and intimate history with God.

Building this altar was a way for Jacob to show thankfulness to God for His providence and protective care. The God of the universe is always at work in our lives. We often fail to show thankfulness for all the little things He does in our lives. Psalm 46:1 says, *"God is our refuge and strength, a very present help in trouble."*

It's so important to influence your children like Abraham and Isaac did for Jacob. When your children grow up and move away, do they immediately look for a church in their new location? Make godly deposits in your children through prayer and devotion at the family altar.

Jacob #2

> **Genesis 35:7**
> **And he built an altar there and called the place El Bethel, because there God appeared to him when he fled from the face of his brother.**

Reason for Building the Altar

So much is going on in this passage, beginning with verse one: God said to Jacob, *"Arise, go up to Bethel and dwell there. Make an altar there to the God who appeared to you when you fled from your brother Esau."*

Jacob directed his household to put away their idols and foreign gods and purify themselves (vv 2-4). Even though Jacob knew who the one true God was, he had allowed his household to follow other idol gods. He knew he was going to Bethel to meet with God and that the condition of his household was unacceptable.

Jacob built an altar and called the place El-bethel – the "God of the house of God" (v 7). Isn't that an incredible revelation of Yahweh? He is the God of the house of God! God is always concerned about His house – His people. All that He does in the earth is for the purpose of building His people. This was true in the Old Testament and it is certainly true under the New Covenant.

God appeared to Jacob and changed his name to Israel and once more reaffirmed His promise to Abraham and Isaac.

> **Genesis 35:10-12**
> **10 And God said to him, "Your name is Jacob; your name shall not be called Jacob anymore, but Israel shall be your name." So He called his name Israel.**

11 Also God said to him: "I am God Almighty. Be fruitful and multiply; a nation and a company of nations shall proceed from you, and kings shall come from your body.

12 The land which I gave Abraham and Isaac I give to you; and to your descendants after you I give this land."

Spiritual Application

Remember the house of God and the God of the house of God. Even though salvation comes through a personal relationship with Jesus, God's ultimate plan for the ages is to have a family. That family is called the church. Being saved means being baptized into the body of Christ. This means that we are no longer individual members exclusive of one another. Rather we are interdependent of one another.

We are never to neglect gathering together as the body of Christ.

> **Hebrews 10:25 Not forsaking the assembling of ourselves together, as is the manner of some, but exhorting one another, and so much the more as you see the Day approaching.**

As followers of Jesus, we must purify ourselves from the idols of the heart. Just as Jacob had to purify his household in order to meet with God, we must purify our hearts from the idols of materialism and selfish ambition. Jesus said, *"Blessed are the pure in heart, for they shall see God"* (Matthew 5:8). If we want to have true encounters with God, we must purify ourselves.

As Jacob's name was changed to Israel, we must remember that we are new creations – no longer Jacob (supplanter) but Israel (prince with God).

Chapter 2 Review

1. What was the first altar listed in the Bible?

_____

_____

2. How many altars did Abraham build?

_____

_____

3. What promise did God make to Abraham when he built his first altar?

_____

_____

_____

4. Where Abraham pitched a _____, he built an _____.

5. God remembers His _____ and He forgets our _____.

6. When Jacob built his second altar, what did God change?

_____

Chapter 3: Altar Builders – Part 2, Prophets, Judges & Kings

Moses #1

> **Exodus 17:15**
> **And Moses built an altar and called its name, The-Lord-Is-My-Banner.**

Reason for Building the Altar

Israel fought with Amalek while in the wilderness. Moses went to the top of the hill with the rod of God in his hand and when he held up his hand, Israel prevailed. When Moses let down his hand, Amalek prevailed. Aaron and Hur held up Moses' hands and Israel won the battle (vv 8-13).

God told Moses that He would utterly blot out the name of Amalek from under heaven and Moses built an altar there and called its name Yahweh-Nissi – the

Lord our Banner (v 15). Other than Jacob's (El Elohe Israel, Genesis 33:20), no other altars were given names.

We might imagine the banner in reference was like a flag, as this is how banners are thought of today. But the banner of armies during this time period was an unbending pole that had an ornament of bright metal on the top. The banner-pole spoken of was very much like the rod in Moses' hand. His rod was similar to a small banner. When he lifted it, victory came to Israel, but when it dropped, the enemy prevailed.

Spiritual Application

The battle we face as believers is very real. We must remember that the battle belongs to the Lord. Like Moses raising the banner of his rod, when we allow the Lord to fight our battle by trusting in Him, we prevail. When we allow fear and worry to dominate our minds, we become defeated.

While the battle in Exodus 17 was with a physical enemy, our warfare is spiritual in nature. It often manifests through natural channels, but the source of the opposition is the kingdom of darkness.

> **Ephesians 6:12 For we do not wrestle against flesh and blood, but against principalities, against powers, against the rulers of the darkness of this age, against spiritual hosts of wickedness in the heavenly places.**

Just as Moses needed the help of Aaron and Hur, we need one another – we can't do it on our own. The Christian must never fight alone. This is Satan's strategy – to isolate the believer. In doing so, Satan gains the advantage. It is important to have people like Aaron and Hur in your life, especially if you are in any type of leadership role.

The Lord is our Banner under which victory is certain.

Moses #2

> **Exodus 24:4**
> **And Moses wrote all the words of the Lord. And he rose early in the morning, and built an altar at the foot of the mountain, and twelve pillars according to the twelve tribes of Israel.**

Reason for Building the Altar

The altar was built to offer sacrifices that would be the blood of the Mosaic Covenant. Moses selected 12 pillars (long stones) to represent the 12 tribes of Israel to build the altar. This signified that Yahweh was entering a covenant with Israel.

After the sacrifices, Moses read the book of the covenant in the ears of the people and they responded that they would be obedient and do all that the Lord commanded (v 7).

Spiritual Application

No covenant is binding without the shedding of blood. The word *covenant* means "to make an incision – where the blood flows." We are now under the New Covenant, which Jesus cut with the Father on the cross. For that covenant to fail, Jesus would have to fail – and He never fails.

The Bible is clear that without the shedding of blood there's no remission of sin.

> **Hebrews 9:22 And according to the law almost all things are purified with blood, and without shedding of blood there is no remission.**

Old Testament sacrifices could never remove sin. The blood of bulls and goats would temporarily cover the sins of God's people, insomuch as it symbolized the blood of Jesus. But only when the fulfillment of the type and symbol came – Jesus – could sin be removed.

Balaam

> **Numbers 23:1, 14, 29**
> **1 Then Balaam said to Balak, "Build seven altars for me here, and prepare for me here seven bulls and seven rams."**
> **14 So he brought him to the field of Zophim, to the top of Pisgah, and built seven altars, and offered a bull and a ram on each altar.**
> **29 Then Balaam said to Balak, "Build for me here seven altars, and prepare for me here seven bulls and seven rams."**

Reason for Building the Altar

On three different occasions, Balak, the king of Moab, inquired of Balaam to bring a curse upon Israel. Balaam built altars and offered sacrifices on each occasion and queried the Lord. Balaam is one of the most interesting characters in the Old Testament. It seems that Balaam was following a superstitious formula with the offerings in order to get a word from God. It is questionable what kind of personal relationship he had with God.

Each time, the message from God was clear: *One cannot curse what God has blessed* (Numbers 23:8, 20; 24:9).

Spiritual Application

Balaam was trying to use, what appeared to be, a superstitious formula to invoke God. Lots of Christians today make similar efforts to get God's attention – following rituals and traditions in the place of personal relationship. There is no substitute for personal relationship.

The New Testament tell us that if God be for you then who can be against you (Romans 8:31). This is similar to the declaration that one cannot curse what God has blessed. So many Christians are worried about witches and warlocks placing curses on them, but if the blood of Jesus covers you and God is for you, there is no need to fear.

Tucked away in this chapter is the statement that *"God is not a man, that He should lie"* (23:19). It is impossible for God to lie. The truth of God's Word is forever settled in heaven (Psalm 119:89). There is not even a shadow of turning in God (James 1:17).

God doesn't see our past sin when He looks at us.

Numbers 23:21 He [God] has not observed iniquity in Jacob, nor has He seen wickedness in Israel. The LORD his God is with him, and the shout of a King is among them.

When God looks at you, He sees the righteousness of God in Christ (2 Corinthians 5:21).

Joshua

Deuteronomy 27:4-7
4 Therefore it shall be, when you have crossed over the Jordan, that on Mount Ebal you shall set up these stones, which I command you today, and you shall whitewash them with lime.
5 And there you shall build an altar to the Lord your God, an altar of stones; you shall not use an iron tool on them.
6 You shall build with whole stones the altar of the Lord your God, and offer burnt offerings on it to the Lord your God.
7 You shall offer peace offerings, and shall eat there, and rejoice before the Lord your God.
8 And you shall write very plainly on the stones all the words of this law."

Reason for Building the Altar

The context for Joshua building this altar was the crossing over the Jordan River. This represented new beginnings. The Ten Commandments were to be written on these stones to remind Israel of their covenant with God. It took Israel forty years to make this crossing. This was due to unbelief in the hearts of the Israelites. Again and again they tested God in the wilderness with their unbelief.

According to God's plan, the journey should have taken two years. Not because that's how long the physical distance required – that was less than a month, but because that's how long the spiritual distance required. The Israelites needed to learn the ways of God, receive the Law, build the Tabernacle and establish the divine order of worship. All they'd ever know was slavery and they needed their minds renewed before entering the Promised Land.

Notice that the tools of men – i.e., iron tools were not to be used on this altar. This is also per God's instructions in Exodus 20:25, "If you make me an altar of stone, you shall not build it of hewn stones, for if you wield your tool on it you profane it" (ESV).

Spiritual Application

The New Covenant is primarily about new beginnings. "If anyone is in Christ, he is a new creation; old things have passed away; behold, all things have become new" (2 Corinthians 5:17). But like the Israelites, after our conversion, we need time to renew our minds with the truth of God's Word (Romans 12:2).

We need to setup spiritual altars – places of consecration, that remind us of what God's Word says about our lives. We come into our relationship with God with all sorts of emotional and mental baggage. Some of it is immediately dealt with through the new birth, but other parts are worked through in the sanctification process as we allow God to change us from the inside out.

As it relates to our worship, God forbids the embellishment and polish of men. The Lord looks solely on the unhewn heart of man, and none to the outward adornment. John 4:24 says, "God is Spirit, and those who worship Him must worship in spirit and truth."

Gideon

Judges 6:26-27

26 build an altar to the Lord your God on top of this rock in the proper arrangement, and take the second bull and offer a burnt sacrifice with the wood of the image which you shall cut down."

27 So Gideon took ten men from among his servants and did as the Lord had said to him. But because he feared his father's household and the men of the city too much to do it by day, he did it by night.

Reason for Building the Altar

Israel had come into servitude to the Midianites for a period of seven years. In their oppression, Israel cried out to God to deliver them. God sent them a prophet to remind them that He was the same God who had delivered them out of Egypt. Afterwards, the Angel of the Lord appeared to Gideon and said, "The Lord is with you, you mighty man of valor!" But Gideon wanted to know why the Lord had allowed all of the bad things to happen.

Judges 6:13 Gideon said to Him, "O my lord, if the Lord is with us, why then has all this

happened to us? And where are all His miracles which our fathers told us about, saying, 'Did not the Lord bring us up from Egypt?' But now the Lord has forsaken us and delivered us into the hands of the Midianites."

The Lord answered Gideon, "Go in this might of yours, and you shall save Israel from the hand of the Midianites. Have I not sent you?"

First, Gideon built an altar after his encounter with God and called it *The-Lord-is-Peace,* or Yahweh-Shalom (v 24). It would seem that there was no sacrifice placed on this altar, but rather it was built as a monument to memorialize this divine meeting.

In verse 25, Gideon was told by the Lord to tear down the altar to Baal that his father had erected and to offer his father's second bullock, seven years old, to the Lord. It isn't explained why the second, but perhaps the first was already prepared for Baal and the second was the only one fit for the Lord. Gideon was also ordered to cut down the grove next to it and use the wood from it to sacrifice a burnt offering to the Lord.

Because Gideon knew the consequences of such actions – destroying the altar to Baal, he enlisted the aid of ten of his servants. When the men of the city arose the next morning and saw that the altar to Baal was torn down they were enraged and determined to kill Gideon. But the Bible says that the Spirit of the Lord was upon Gideon (v 34). It was then that Gideon set a fleece before the Lord and received confirmation of the Lord's deliverance.

Gideon built this altar at night. Things would drastically be changed for Israel after that night. This altar represented that the false god of Baal no longer had control in Israel.

Spiritual Application

The child of God cannot serve two masters. Just as Elijah proclaimed, "How long will you falter between two opinions? If the Lord *is* God, follow Him; but if Baal, follow him" (1 Kings 18:21). When a person has been under spiritual oppression, the only way to break free from the bondage is to tear down the idols of the heart and build an altar of consecration to the Lord in its place.

Gideon felt that he was the last one to be qualified to be the deliver of Israel. God does not call the qualified, but qualifies the called. God may have some great work for your life and He is simply looking for obedience.

Samuel

> **1 Samuel 7:17 But he always returned to Ramah, for his home was there. There he judged Israel, and there he built an altar to the LORD.**

Reason for Building the Altar

Ramah was Samuel's home. His office as a prophet and judge took him many places throughout the land of Israel, but he always returned home to Ramah. It was from there that he judged Israel. Samuel knew that he could not administer justice without the intervention of God, thus he built an altar there to honor Yahweh and remind himself of his continual need for God's presence and direction.

The Ark of the Covenant had been taken captive by the Philistines in chapter four. Due to the calamities they were struck with, the Philistines sent the Ark back to Israel in chapter six. But the Ark was not placed back in the tabernacle; instead it was in private custody. Thus, Samuel chose his home to be the place to make an offering unto Yahweh.

Spiritual Application

There will be times when our normal patterns of worship are disrupted. In the spring of 2020 there was a great disruption of normal activity due to the spread of the Corona Virus. This especially impacted the Christian community, as gatherings were restricted. Gatherings were relegated to online services and the home became the focal point in our spiritual lives. In those types of situations where you cannot gather and worship as normal, make an altar wherever you are. God is not limited to a building. The sacrifices with which God is pleased are a broken and a contrite spirit (Psalm 51:17).

Moreover, as judge, Samuel needed God's wisdom and direction. As followers of Jesus, we need His continual guidance. As we build altars of devotion to the Lord, He opens up our spiritual hearing. The family altar at home is the most crucial altar because our families are our greatest responsibility.

As an aside, but related to Samuel, it's interesting to note the outcome of Samuel's two sons compared to Eli's. When he was old Samuel appointed his sons as judges, but the Bible records the following: *But his sons did not walk in his ways; they turned aside after dishonest gain, took bribes, and perverted justice* (1 Samuel 8:3). The interesting part is that Eli didn't raise his sons properly in the ways of the Lord, but Samuel did. In the end, the result was the same. I say this not to discourage, but as a reminder that as parents you can do everything right, but ultimately the choices will belong to your children when they're grown. Do all that you can to train your children in the ways of God, then trust Him to work in their lives – even when they go astray for a season.

Saul

1 Samuel 14:33-35
33 Then they told Saul, saying, "Look, the people are sinning against the LORD by eating with the blood!" So he said, "You have dealt treacherously; roll a large stone to me this day."
34 Then Saul said, "Disperse yourselves among the people, and say to them, 'Bring me here every man's ox and every man's sheep, slaughter them here, and eat; and do not sin against the LORD by eating with the blood.' " So every one of the people brought his ox with him that night, and slaughtered it there.
35 Then Saul built an altar to the LORD. This was the first altar that he built to the LORD.

Reason for Building the Altar

Saul was the people's choice for king. They felt that he was everything they needed to make them just like the other nations around them. In doing so, they were rejecting God as their King. This was the first altar that Saul had built on his own. He did so in panic, hoping that God would intervene in their battle. Saul's heart would ultimately be revealed as rebellious and God took the throne from him.

Saul relied heavily on his own abilities and very little on the Lord's strength. He felt that it was Samuel's job to intercede with God for favor and blessing. Eventually, this mentality led Saul to be more and more presumptive and to disregard God's ways.

Spiritual Application

Some people only get serious with God when there's some type of adversity going on in their lives. Like Saul, they 'get by' just fine on their own under normal circumstances. They rely on others to do all the spiritual heavy lifting. If you look at their lives, they appear to be just like the world around them. In their hearts there's a root of rebellion that will manifest under pressure.

Like Saul, people who get by on their own ability rely on others to shape their spiritual destiny. It's time to take your relationship with God seriously. Building altars when things go wrong is a good start. But if you forget God when things work out, you'll be worse off than when it happened. Build spiritual altars out of love and devotion for your Savior, not just out of fear for the circumstances.

David

> **2 Samuel 24:18-19**
> **18 And Gad came that day to David and said to him, "Go up, erect an altar to the LORD on the threshing floor of Araunah the Jebusite."**
> **19 So David, according to the word of Gad, went up as the LORD commanded.**

Reason for Building the Altar

On an impulse, David took a census of Israel and Judah. The result was that David had an army of 1.3 million soldiers. The census displeased the Lord because it showed that David was putting his trust in the strength of his army and not in the Lord. For this reason, God brought judgment upon Israel in the form of a plague; 70,000 people died in three days. But the Lord relented and did not destroy Jerusalem.

Gad the prophet came to David and gave him a message from God that he was to build an altar to the Lord on the threshing floor of Araunah the Jebusite. Araunah wanted to give the threshing floor to David out of honor, but David's response reveals the heart of worship.

2 Samuel 24:21-25

21 Then Araunah said, "Why has my lord the king come to his servant?" And David said, "To buy the threshing floor from you, to build an altar to the Lord, that the plague may be withdrawn from the people."

22 Now Araunah said to David, "Let my lord the king take and offer up whatever seems good to him. Look, here are oxen for burnt sacrifice, and threshing implements and the yokes of the oxen for wood.

23 All these, O king, Araunah has given to the king." And Araunah said to the king, "May the Lord your God accept you."

24 Then the king said to Araunah, "No, but I will surely buy it from you for a price; nor will I offer burnt offerings to the Lord my God with that which costs me nothing." So David bought the threshing floor and the oxen for fifty shekels of silver.

25 And David built there an altar to the Lord, and offered burnt offerings and peace offerings. So the Lord heeded the prayers for the land, and the plague was withdrawn from Israel.

David's response was, "Nor will I offer burnt offerings to the Lord my God with that which costs me nothing." David built the altar and offered burnt and peace offerings and the Lord withdrew the plague. David was a man after God's own heart, but there were occasions when he missed God and other times when he failed God. When he turned back to God, he did so with all his heart.

Spiritual Application

Even those closest to God will have failures. David was a perfect example of this. When he sinned with Bathsheba (2 Samuel 11), he harbored the sin in his heart for two years, but when he turned back to God he did so with a repentant heart. Psalm 51 is David's prayer at this time: *"Create in me a clean heart, O God, and renew a steadfast spirit within me"* (v 10).

In the matter related to the census, the prophet told David exactly where to build the altar – on the threshing floor of Araunah the Jebusite. Araunah wanted to give the spot to David, but David did not want to offer to the Lord that which cost him nothing, so he bought it. It's important to realize that our worship to God comes with a cost – a sacrifice. It's easy to worship God when everything is going right, but when life is hard we still must offer to God the sacrifice of praise.

> **Habakkuk 3:17-18**
> **17 Though the fig tree may not blossom, Nor fruit be on the vines; Though the labor of the olive may fail, And the fields yield no food; Though the flock may be cut off from the fold, And there be no herd in the stalls—**
> **18 Yet I will rejoice in the LORD, I will joy in the God of my salvation.**

Elijah

> **1 Kings 18:30-32**
> **30 Then Elijah said to all the people, "Come near to me." So all the people came near to him. And he repaired the altar of the Lord that was broken down.**
> **31 And Elijah took twelve stones, according to the number of the tribes of the sons of Jacob, to whom the word of the Lord had come, saying, "Israel shall be your name."**

32 Then with the stones he built an altar in the name of the Lord; and he made a trench around the altar large enough to hold two seahs of seed.

Reason for Building the Altar

Israel was in a state of apostasy. They had forsaken the one true living God and instead worshipped Baal. Ahab was the king and his wife Jezebel had massacred the prophets of the Lord (1 Kings 18:4). Elijah confronted Ahab and called a showdown on Mount Carmel with the 450 prophets of Baal and the 400 prophets of Asherah, a Canaanite goddess.

Neither Elijah nor the false prophets were to put a fire under their offering, but instead call on their respective deity to provide the fire. The false prophets called on Baal to no avail. The idol god could not hear them because he was a false god. Elijah mocked them with comments like, "Maybe he went on vacation" and "Maybe he's asleep."

The prophet of God patiently waited until the false prophets had exhausted themselves then repaired the altar of the Lord and dug a trench around it and filled it with water. This altar may have been built during the time of the Judges, or later by King Saul. But it had become broken down, much like the spiritual condition of God's people.

When Elijah called on the name of Yahweh and He responded.

> **1 Kings 18:37-39**
> **37 Hear me, O Lord, hear me, that this people may know that You are the Lord God, and that You have turned their hearts back to You again."**
> **38 Then the fire of the Lord fell and consumed the burnt sacrifice, and the wood and the stones and the dust, and it licked up the water that was in the trench.**
> **39 Now when all the people saw it, they fell on their faces; and they said, "The Lord, He is God! The Lord, He is God!"**

Elijah then had the false prophets seized and he executed them. The remaining part of the story is that God ended the drought and brought an abundance of rain upon the land.

Spiritual Application

Elijah issued the challenge to God's people, "How long will you falter between two opinions? If the Lord is

God, follow Him; but if Baal, follow him" (1 Kings 18:21). This story of Elijah's showdown with the prophets of Baal reminds us that we cannot serve both God and mammon – the idol of materialism (Matthew 6:24). It is impossible to serve two masters. When we say that God comes first in our lives, do we demonstrate that message with our actions and our priorities? Ultimately, we will be put to the test.

Idolatry happens in modern times much differently than in Bible times. But the root issue is exactly the same. The first commandment is, "You shall have no other gods before Me" (Exodus 20:3). God is a jealous God and He wants all of the idols of the heart to be torn down so that there is no other God but Him in your life. Sometimes the idol in our hearts is the God we have invented in our minds. This fictional God likes everything we like and he hates everything we hate. This is what happens when we don't get our revelation of God from the Bible – the only true source of revelation about God. He is the Author of Scripture. But when we devise this other God in our mind and then that version of God doesn't show up when we want him to, it leaves us angry and disillusioned.

When Elijah repaired the altar of God and the Lord demonstrated His approval by fire, there was an abundance of rain poured out upon a barren land to end the drought. When someone turns back to the Lord in repentance, and in effect, repairs the altar, God pours out the abundance of rain. The Lord is longsuffering and willing to restore if we humbly turn to Him.

Chapter 3 Review

1. What was the occasion for which Moses built his first altar?

_____

_____

_____

2. What is the meaning of the word *covenant*?

_____

_____

3. What was Balaam doing in order to get a word from God?

_____

_____

4. What sin did David commit that led up to him building an altar?

_____

5. What happened in the land after Elijah repaired the altar and God consumed the offering by fire?

_____

_____

Chapter 4: Memorials

Before the Israelites entered the Promised Land, God told them to set up a memorial of their deliverance from slavery and their arrival to the land that God promised their forefather Abraham. They were to do so by erecting 12 stones taken from the middle of the Jordan River, which they'd just miraculously crossed over on dry ground.

> **Joshua 4:1-7**
> **And it came to pass, when all the people had completely crossed over the Jordan, that the Lord spoke to Joshua, saying:**
> **2 "Take for yourselves twelve men from the people, one man from every tribe,**
> **3 and command them, saying, 'Take for yourselves twelve stones from here, out of the midst of the Jordan, from the place where the priests' feet stood firm. You shall carry them over with you and leave them in the lodging place where you lodge tonight.'"**

4 Then Joshua called the twelve men whom he had appointed from the children of Israel, one man from every tribe;

5 and Joshua said to them: "Cross over before the ark of the Lord your God into the midst of the Jordan, and each one of you take up a stone on his shoulder, according to the number of the tribes of the children of Israel,

6 that this may be a sign among you when your children ask in time to come, saying, 'What do these stones mean to you?'

7 Then you shall answer them that the waters of the Jordan were cut off before the ark of the covenant of the Lord; when it crossed over the Jordan, the waters of the Jordan were cut off. And these stones shall be for a memorial to the children of Israel forever."

This was the second time that Israel miraculously crossed over a body of water on dry ground. The first instance was in Exodus 14 in their deliverance from Egypt. Both of these scenarios are very analogous to the Christian life. You can't have the entrance into the Promised Land without the deliverance out of Egypt. In other words, you cannot live an everyday victorious Christian life unless your first get delivered from the bondage of sin.

"These stones shall be for a memorial to the children of Israel forever."

The Hebrew word for *memorial* (*zikkaron*) means *reminder*. Memorials help us to remember the great things God has done for us. They also help us to teach future generations about the faithfulness of God. Sometimes in the heat of the battle our judgment gets clouded and we begin to doubt God's faithfulness. A memorial serves as reminder that God is with us in the battle and will never fail us.

It's so important what we remember; equally so, what we forget. Too often we build memorials to the things we are supposed to forget. We fill our lives with reminders of past failures and wonder why we keep repeating the same poor behaviors. Instead, we need to fill our lives with reminders of God's goodness and faithfulness. The seven feasts of the Lord were all reminders of the steadfast love and faithfulness of Yahweh.

The Seven Feasts of the Lord - Reminders

Passover (Exodus 12:1-4): A reminder of the night they were delivered out of Egypt, when the destroyer passed over them because of the blood of the lamb on the doorposts and lintels of their homes. Prophetically, this feast points towards Jesus on the cross.

Unleavened Bread (Exodus 12:15-20): The bread was made in a hurry. So this is a reminder of how the Lord brought the Israelites out of Egypt in haste. Prophetically, this feast points towards the burial of our Lord.

Firstfruits (Leviticus 23:9-14): Israelites offered the firstfruits of barley to the Lord as a way of dedicating the entire harvest to Him. Our Lord was raised from the dead on Firstfruits. Prophetically, this feast points towards the resurrection. This is a reminder that Jesus is the first of many who will be raised at the resurrection.

Pentecost (Leviticus 23:23-25): The Law of Moses was given on Pentecost – 50 days after Passover. Prophetically, this feast points to when the Holy Spirit would be poured out. The Holy Spirit was poured out on the day of Pentecost and the church was born (Acts 2). This feast serves as a reminder that the Holy Spirit is always with us.

Feast of Trumpets (Leviticus 23:23-25): This feast was the beginning of a new year. Prophetically, the Feast of Trumpets points to the rapture of the church (1 Thessalonians 4). We are reminded that there is a new day coming when the trump of God sounds (1 Thessalonians 4:16).

Day of Atonement (Leviticus 23:26-32): The High Priest would enter the Holy of Holies once a year on this day and sprinkle the blood of the animal sacrifice upon the Mercy Seat of the Ark. I doing so, the sin of Israel would be covered for another year. A living scapegoat would also be released into the wilderness as a sign that their sins had been carried away. Jesus on the cross is the fulfillment of our Atonement. He shed His blood, once and for all, for our redemption. Now, believers may enter God's presence at all times. We remember the great price that He paid through the observance of Holy Communion. Prophetically, this feast points towards the Second Coming.

Feast of Tabernacles (Leviticus 23:33-43): This feast commemorates the 40-year wilderness journey. It's a week-long celebration to remember how Israel lived under God's care during their wilderness wanderings. Booths, or temporary shelters made with branches were built as memorials. Prophetically, this feast points towards God's eternal kingdom.

Each of these seven feasts serve as reminders of what God has done. But they also speak prophetically of what was to come. This is very much how memorials and altars work. They serve as reminders of encounters with God or blessings from God, but they also point us forward to greater things to come in God's plan.

The Lord's Supper

The greatest memorial of all is the Lord's Supper. It's the ultimate reminder of the price our Lord paid on the cross for our salvation.

> **1 Corinthians 11:23-26**
> **23 For I received from the Lord that which I also delivered to you: that the Lord Jesus on the same night in which He was betrayed took bread;**
> **24 and when He had given thanks, He broke it and said, "Take, eat; this is My body which is broken for you; do this in remembrance of Me."**
> **25 In the same manner He also took the cup after supper, saying, "This cup is the new covenant in My blood. This do, as often as you drink it, in remembrance of Me."**
> **26 For as often as you eat this bread and drink this cup, you proclaim the Lord's death till He comes.**

We eat from the bread and drink from the cup in remembrance of the body and blood of our Lord. Let's examine these memorial elements.

The Bread

Bread represents life. Jesus said in John 6:51 that He was the Bread of Life and that if any man would eat of that bread, he would live forever. When Jesus broke the bread, He signified that His body was going to be broken for us, that we might have life and life more abundantly.

The broken body of Jesus also represents the tearing of the veil of the temple. Matthew 27:51 says the when Jesus died on the Cross that the veil that kept man separated from the Holy of Holies was torn in two – from top to bottom. The tearing from the top represents that it was God Who tore the veil in response to the death of Christ on the Cross.

The veil was 30 feet wide, 60 feet high and three inches thick! Because of the broken body of our Lord, we now have access to the throne room of God 24/7.

We also know that part of the brokenness of our Lord's body were the 39 stripes that He took for our healing. 1 Peter 2:24 says that "by His stripes we were healed." We partake of the bread in remembrance of the Lord's broken body. Paul also said that we proclaim the Lord's death during this act of partaking. The way that we remember and proclaim the Lord's death and the breaking of His body is by partaking of the benefits of His broken body. Healing is *the children's bread*. Jesus said this to the Syrophoenician woman in reference to the Abrahamic covenant (Matthew 15:26), but now we have a better covenant, established on better promises.

If you are sick in body, as you partake of the element of the bread, thank Jesus for taking the 39 stripes on His back for your healing. Receive by faith the healing virtue of Jesus into your body. Stand on God's Word that your body will proclaim and demonstrate the death of Jesus on the Cross by receiving all of the benefits of the Cross.

The Cup

The cup of grape juice or wine (either may be used) represents the blood of Jesus. This is the same blood that was used to cut covenant with the Father and secure our eternal inheritance. The cup represents the suffering of our Lord. Jesus said, "The cup which My Father has given Me, shall I not drink it?" (John 18:11). By partaking of the cup, we are making the commitment that we will follow Jesus, no matter what the cost.

In Matthew 26:28, *"For this is My blood of the new covenant, which is shed for many for the remission of sins."* Partaking of the fruit of the vine in Holy Communion is to identify with Jesus in his cutting of the covenant. We are saying that everything that we have belongs to God and remembering that everything God has belongs to us. Paul also referred to it as the "cup of blessing" in 1 Corinthians 10:16. All of the blessings of the blood covenant belong to the child of God.

A Second Set of Stones

Let's look back at the story in Joshua. Although there was no memorial built for the first miracle at the Red Sea, there was a second memorial of 12 stones erected at the bottom of the Jordan River.

> **Joshua 4:9 Then Joshua set up twelve stones in the midst of the Jordan, in the place where the feet of the priests who bore the ark of the covenant stood; and they are there to this day.**

It is never explicitly stated why this second memorial was constructed below the waters of the Jordan. One possibility is that these stones were placed there as a reminder of those who didn't make it over. Many Israelites who came out of Egypt died in the wilderness because of their unbelief in the ability of God to bring them into the Promised Land. They thought that the giants of Canaan were too formidable to overcome.

As you walk out your relationship with God, the goal is to live this life victoriously. Our lives should be examples of God's delivering power. Which set of 12 stones do you want to represent your life – the ones at the bottom of the Jordan or the ones in the Promised Land? The choice is entirely yours. Will your stones represent the many who gave up or will they testify of God's goodness in your life?

Chapter 4 Review

1. What does the Hebrew word for *memorial* mean?

_____

_____

2. Which of the seven feasts remind us that Jesus is the first of many who will be raised at the resurrection.?

_____

_____

3. What is the greatest memorial of all?

_____

_____

4. What does the broken body of our Lord represent?

_____

5. What did the second set of stones represent?

_____

_____

_____

_____

Chapter 5: Old Testament Sacrifices

Under the Old Covenant, the blood of animals was used for the atonement of the people of Israel. The word atonement, however, only means "to cover" and not to remove. The blood of bulls and goats could not take away sin. But it was a *type* of the blood of Christ. Each and every sacrifice under the Old Covenant was symbolic of the sacrifice of Jesus on the cross.

People under the Old Covenant were saved by *looking forward* to the Cross (through the type) just as we are saved by *looking back* to the Cross.

Below are the Old Testament animal sacrifices and how each one represented the redemptive work of Christ. Each of these sacrifices is described in detail in the Book of Leviticus chapters one through six. These sacrifices were made at the Tabernacle of Moses, and later at the Temple of Solomon.

This is a drawing of the Tabernacle of Moses.

Burnt Offering

The burnt offering was wholly consumed and symbolized that Jesus was completely obedient unto the death of the Cross. Philippians 2:8 says, *"And being found in appearance as a man, He humbled Himself and became obedient to the point of death, even the death of the cross."* Jesus was wholly consumed as our burnt offering.

The Hebrew word for "burnt offering" (Heb. *olah*) means "that which goes up," literally to "go up in smoke." The smoke from the burnt offering ascended to God, "a sweet aroma to the LORD."

> **Leviticus 1:9 And the priest shall burn all on the altar as a burnt sacrifice, an offering made by fire, a sweet aroma to the LORD.**

It was a sweet aroma to the Lord because it represented Christ offering up Himself to God. The sacrifice of Jesus was a sweet-smelling aroma because it secured redemption for God's creation.

> **Ephesians 5:2 And walk in love, as Christ also has loved us and given Himself for us, an offering and a sacrifice to God for a sweet-smelling aroma.**

The Israelites would bring a male sheep, bull, or goat with no defect to the entrance of the tabernacle and kill it. The animal's blood was drained and the priest would sprinkle the blood around the altar. The animal was skinned and cut it into pieces. The priest would burn the pieces over the altar all night. Afterwards, the priest would receive the skin as payment for his services.

Sin Offering

The sin offering was made when there was no possible restitution. The Law was given that the whole world might stand guilty of sin before God. There was no possible restitution that man could make. We were all condemned. Jesus took the sin of the whole world upon Himself. 2 Corinthians 5:21 says, *"For He made Him who knew no sin to be sin for us, that we might become the righteousness of God in Him."* Jesus was made to be sin for us. This means that He was made to be the sin offering, not that he partook of the sin nature, as some have taught.

The sin offering was made for sins committed in ignorance or were unintentional sins. The Hebrews language used different words for sin, with different meanings.

Hebrew Word	Meaning
Pesha	"Rebellion or disobedience"
Chataah	"Missing the mark" This is unintentional sin committed in ignorance.
Avon	"Perversion; To deliberately twist and distorting God's word and will for selfish ends."

The word *chataah* is used for sin offerings.

Leviticus 4:2-3
2 "Speak to the children of Israel, saying: 'If a person sins [Heb. chataah] unintentionally against any of the commandments of the Lord in anything which ought not to be done, and does any of them,
3 if the anointed priest sins, bringing guilt on the people, then let him offer to the Lord for his sin [Heb. chataah] which he has sinned a young bull without blemish as a sin [Heb. chataah] offering.

Everyone has sinned and come short of the glory of God (Romans 3:23). It is not normal for a Spirit-filled believer to commit sins of rebellion or perverting the Word of God. But, it is quite common to commit unintentional sin – those thoughts, attitudes, words and actions that we didn't premeditate. Jesus remains our Sin Offering and washes us with His blood as we walk in the light, in fellowship with Him.

1 John 1:7-9
7 But if we walk in the light as He is in the light, we have fellowship with one another, and the blood of Jesus Christ His Son cleanses us from all sin.

8 If we say that we have no sin, we deceive ourselves, and the truth is not in us.

9 If we confess our sins, He is faithful and just to forgive us our sins and to cleanse us from all unrighteousness.

It's never God's will that we sin. But when we do, we have an Advocate with the Father in Jesus Christ, the Righteous One (1 John 2:1). He is our Sin Offering.

Trespass Offering

The trespass offering was made when restitution was required along with the animal sacrifice. As our trespass offering, Jesus made restitution with the Father on our behalf. We have been reconciled to the Father by the blood of Jesus! 2 Corinthians 5:19 says, *"God was in Christ reconciling the world to Himself, not imputing their trespasses to them, and has committed to us the word of reconciliation."*

In a trespass offering, the ram or male lamb was slaughtered and the blood was splashed on the altar. Some of the blood was then applied to the right ear lobe, right thumb, and right big toe of the one making the offering. Most of the sacrificial animal was burned; however, the priests were able to eat some portions while they were in the sanctuary. Oil was also applied to the right ear lobe, right thumb, right big toe and the head of the one making the offering.

Jesus teaches the principle of restitution and reconciliation in the Sermon on the Mount.

> **Matthew 5:23-24**
> **23 Therefore if you bring your gift to the altar, and there remember that your brother has something against you,**
> **24 leave your gift there before the altar, and go your way. First be reconciled to your brother, and then come and offer your gift.**

Jesus paid the full price for our sins on the cross. However, that does not mean that we should never make amends for our wrongdoing. Although not applicable in every situation, allow the Holy Spirit to guide you when this is needed. A good rule of thumb when *not* to do this is when doing so makes you feel better but makes the other person feel horrible – if there is no other greater good being served. There once was a man in one of the churches I pastored who confessed to his wife (in front of the whole church) that he had been thinking all week how ugly she was. He wanted her to forgive him. Needless to say, that situation did not end well and he ended up walking home that night.

Unless it also helps the other party (e.g., restores lost or stolen property) or serves some greater good, confess your sin to God and leave it at the foot of the cross.

Peace Offering

The peace offering was frequently offered with the burnt offering. Parts of it were eaten by the priest and the worshipper. As believers, we share in Jesus' work on the Cross. Jesus said in John 6:54, *"Whosoever eats my flesh, and drinks my blood, has eternal life; and I will raise him up at the last day."* We are partakers of all the Jesus did on the Cross.

There were three situations where a peace offering was made:

1. For purposes of thanksgiving – as an expression of worship.
2. As part of a fulfilled vow.
3. As praise for God's deliverance out of a dire situation.

Ephesians 2:14 For He Himself is our peace.

Meal Offering

The meal offering was a non-blood offering. It represents the earth-walk of Christ. For 33½ years, Jesus lived a perfect, sinless life. He was the Lamb of God without blemish. Hebrews 4:15 says, *"He was in all points tempted as we are, yet without sin."* Jesus was only able to offer His blood on the cross because He lived a perfect life without sin.

A meal offering would have most likely been one of wheat or barley, depending on what was available. When a person brought a meal offering to the priests, a small portion of it was offered to God, with some frankincense, on the altar. The rest of the meal offering went to the priests.

How the meal offering was prepared:

- **The flour was mingled with oil.** The humanity of Jesus was under the power of the Holy Spirit.
- **Frankincense was poured upon it.** The life of Christ was a sweet aroma to the Father.
- **It was seasoned with salt.** Salt seasons and preserves. Additionally, it kills contaminants.

Following Jesus will season us, preserve us and rid us of the contaminant of sin.
- **No leaven or honey was to be added.** The life of Jesus was not one puffed up (leaven) or embellished (honey). As we seek to live His life, we must do so in the same manner.

It is so important to remember that all of these sacrifices were merely types of symbols of the one final and perfect sacrifice – the Lord Jesus Christ on the cross. The Old Testament sacrifices could never remove sin; there remained a constant reminder within the conscience. Only the blood of Jesus can cleanse a person's conscience.

> **Hebrews 10:3-4**
> **3 But in those sacrifices there is a reminder of sins every year.**
> **4 For it is not possible that the blood of bulls and goats could take away sins.**

After the death, burial and resurrection of Jesus, the Jewish religion continued. Offerings were still being made in the Temple. But in 70 A.D. God brought judgment upon the Temple and it was destroyed by the Romans. It was God's way of saying that there is only one sacrifice that is acceptable to Him. Some have proposed that the future temple will resume animal sacrifices in God's eternal kingdom. This is taken from Ezekiel's vision of the future temple. However, this must be seen as figurative as the Bible is clear that there is no other blood sacrifice that will ever be acceptable to Him after His Son's sacrifice on the cross.

Jesus said on the cross (John 19:30):

"It is finished!"

Chapter 5 Review

1. People under the Old Covenant were saved by _____ to the Cross, just as we are saved by _____ to the Cross.

2. What did each Old Testament animal sacrifice represent?

_____

_____

3. What does the Bible mean when it says *"He made Him who knew no sin to be sin for us"*?

_____

_____

_____

4. Which type of sin means "missing the mark" and what would an example be?

_____

_____

_____

5. On the cross, Jesus said, "It is _____."

Chapter 6: The Believer's Altar

The New Testament Altar of Sacrifice

> **Romans 12:1 I beseech you therefore, brethren, by the mercies of God, that you present your bodies a living sacrifice, holy, acceptable to God, which is your reasonable service.**

Here in this verse, we are beseeched or summoned by the mercies of God to bring our sacrifice to the Lord. The Greek word for *beseech* is *parakaleó*, which means, "Called along side to help." The living sacrifice of our lives must be aided by God's mercy. The human will and determination are not enough to kill all that is self and lay it on the altar. It takes God's inexhaustible mercy to accomplish this.

God considers this sacrifice both holy and acceptable in His sight. The Old Testament sacrificial animal had to be without blemish or it was unacceptable. In the New Testament, the sacrifice of one's self on the altar of God can only accomplish this through the blood of Jesus Christ. The use of the word body here in this verse is encompassing of the entire person. The body just so happens to be the weakest link and most likely to resist. If you can harness the body in obedience, the soul will come also. The body is the part of us that most wants to sin. To deny its desires and yield it to God is indeed acceptable in His sight.

As printed, the New King James renders it "your reasonable service." The English Standard Version (ESV) puts it this way: "your spiritual worship."

Now, Romans 12:1 deals with the body – the part of you that most wants to sin. But in the very next verse, Paul deals with the mind – the part of you that most wants to live in the past. It accomplishes very little if you present your body to God but fail to renew your mind with God's Word. The renewing of the mind is the process whereby we are able to discern the perfect will of God for our lives.

> **Romans 12:2 And do not be conformed to this world, but be transformed by the renewing of your mind, that you may prove what is that good and acceptable and perfect will of God.**

Tents and Altars

Like the patriarchs, wherever your tent is, there needs to be an altar to the Lord. People often use the expression that God comes first, then family, then... (fill in the blank). But how often is this really true? From a pastor's point of view, I'm going to say not very often. Of course there must be a healthy balance, but whenever you put family ahead of God you are actually doing your family a disservice. One of my favorite verses is Matthew 6:33, which speaks of priorities.

> **Matthew 6:33 But seek first the kingdom of God and His righteousness, and all these things shall be added to you.**

Some parents like to allow their underage children decide for themselves if they want to go to church. My question to those using that approach is do you let your children decide if they want to go to school? Of course not! Isn't the education of God at least as important as algebra? An even worse scenario is when the children want to go to church and the parents keep making excuses not to go. God will hold parents accountable for raising our children in His ways, to the best of our abilities. You cannot make your children serve Jesus when they grow up, but you can sure push them the other way by failing to lead by example.

Listen to the words of Joshua:

> **Joshua 24:15 And if it seems evil to you to serve the LORD, choose for yourselves this day whom you will serve, whether the gods which your fathers served that were on the other side of the River, or the gods of the Amorites, in whose land you dwell. But as for me and my house, we will serve the LORD.**

"As for me and my house, we will serve the Lord."

It's important that young people have as many personal encounters with God as possible. When they go to Youth Camp and come back fired up for Jesus, it might wear off in a few weeks, but that wasn't time wasted. If they had an encounter with God it will stay with them their entire life. Those personal encounters become like memorial altars in their hearts. When they face a crisis, they will remember that they can turn to a living God who hears and cares.

Encounters

Building alters often resulted from having an encounter with the Lord. God still has encounters with people in today's world – supernatural encounters. When you feel the presence of God, it's undeniable. There is no amount of debate that can dissuade a person who has had an encounter with the living God. When I was twenty years of age I had such an encounter with God. I was lost and in a very dark place. I had been on drugs and alcohol since I was fifteen and was chronically depressed. I was increasingly suicidal. One night God encountered me in a way that felt irresistible. He saved me and delivered me in an instant.

When I was baptized with the Holy Spirit was another such encounter that changed my life forever. I had been saved for a few months and was growing in the Lord, but I was having difficulty finding a Bible-believing church. I went to a Christian counseling seminar at a church on the other end of town one Friday night. After the guest speaker concluded we divided into small groups and prayed for one another. Soon after we started praying it felt like I'd grabbed a live high-voltage wire. Power was surging through my entire being. I began praying in other tongues as they did on the day of Pentecost (Acts 2). Until that day, I'd been very timid and shy about sharing Jesus, but immediately I had a confidence and boldness in sharing the gospel with others.

> **Acts 1:8 But you shall receive power when the Holy Spirit has come upon you; and you shall be witnesses to Me in Jerusalem, and in all Judea and Samaria, and to the end of the earth.**

Worship

Building an altar in the sense of being a living sacrifice means living a lifestyle of worship to God. Some think of worship only in the terms of singing songs at church, but worship is so much more than that. All that we do, when done unto the Lord, is an act of worship. The act of worship must be integrated into the daily life of the believer.

The sacrifice of praise is something that's not based upon an emotional feeling. If we only praise God when we feel Him then we are not truly praising God, but the *feeling* of God. The sacrifice of praise is something that must be offered continually.

> **Hebrews 13:15 Therefore by Him let us continually offer the sacrifice of praise to God,**

that is, the fruit of our lips, giving thanks to His name.

Being a living sacrifice, as Romans 12:1 states, is our spiritual worship.

Consecration

Altars were places of consecration to the Lord. In the life of a believer there will be many occasions when we are called to go deeper, to go further. Jesus repeatedly "upped the ante" with the twelve disciples. He started with "Come and see" (John 1:39) and ultimately the disciples laid down their lives for Jesus. But there were many other points of consecration in between.

Consecrate is mainly an Old Testament word, put it's meaning is prominent in the New Testament. Forty-five of its 73 usages are found in Exodus, Leviticus and Numbers. The Hebrew word (*qadash*) means, "To sanctify, prepare, dedicate, be hallowed, be holy, be sanctified, be separate." Under the Law, this was mostly an outward act, but under the New Covenant, it mostly deals with the heart and the inward condition.

Covenant

We often build spiritual altars at times when we are making vows or covenants with God. In a crisis, we plead with God to intervene. We may also make a vow to the Lord that if He does intervene, we will perform a certain act or lay something down.

Jesus condemned the use of making vows with the intention of finding loopholes (Matthew 5:33-37). Often people forget their vows or find a loophole to not fulfill them, after God intervenes in their crisis. It's important to not make flippant oaths and vows like, "I'll swear on a stack of Bibles" or "I swear on my mother's life." These are the types of meaningless vows that Jesus was condemning.

If you make a vow or a covenant with God, it's important that you follow through and keep it. Understand though that God is not in the deal making business. He wants our hearts not our deals.

Forgiveness

Jesus teaches the principle of forgiveness in the Sermon on the Mount.

Matthew 5:23-24

23 Therefore if you bring your gift to the altar, and there remember that your brother has something against you,

24 leave your gift there before the altar, and go your way. First be reconciled to your brother, and then come and offer your gift.

When you come to the altar to repent or consecrate, the Holy Spirit will bring to your remembrance if there is conflict with a brother or sister in the Lord. It's His will that you seek out reconciliation. Unforgiveness is such a blessing blocker in people's lives. It hinders all that God wants to do in a person's life.

Of course, reconciliation requires two people to get on the same page. But forgiveness can be accomplished on your own. Forgiveness is a choice, not a feeling. Forgiveness is a requirement as a Christian, not an option. Forgiveness is accomplished by the mercy of God. Freely we receive and freely we must give.

When building spiritual altars always ask God to reveal to you if there's any unforgiveness in your heart and ask Him to cleanse you from it.

Intercession

To *intercede* means to "plead for another." The Lord is always looking for those who will make up the hedge and stand in the gap (Ezekiel 22:30). Build an altar for your children, your unsaved spouse, your community, your nation or the world. One of my favorite spiritual altars is to intercede for the persecuted church around the world. Every day I start my prayer time by strategically interceding for at least two countries where the church is persecuted. I spend at least twenty minutes there before I move on to other things.

Be a difference maker in the area of intercession. The Bible describes our prayers like incense that burns before the throne of God.

> **Psalm 141:2 May my prayer be set before You like incense, my uplifted hands like the evening offering.**
>
> **Revelation 8:4 And the smoke of the incense, with the prayers of the saints, ascended before God from the angel's hand.**

Those altars of intercession continue to be like incense that burn before the throne of God long after a saint of

God has departed. When a saint of God dies that's not the end of those prayers. That's the power of intercession.

Conclusion

It's my lasting prayer that God has opened your eyes to the importance of living a consecrated life unto the Lord – to be a living sacrifice. Altars made of stone are no longer needed because of the cross, but God still wants to meet with us on the altar in our heart.

Chapter 6 Review

1. Romans 12:1 deals with the body; what does verse 2 deal with?

_____

_____

2. Why is it important for young people to have encounter with God?

_____

_____

_____

3. How is worship more than singing songs at church?

_____

_____

_____

4. What is the meaning of consecrate?

_____

_____

_____

_____

Other Books by David Chapman

All books may be purchased through Amazon

Thy Word: A Devotional Commentary on Psalm 119 Apr 17, 2019
by David A. Chapman
Paperback
$10⁰⁰ ✓prime

Other Formats: Kindle Edition

The Power of Praise: The 7 Hebrew Words for Praise May 27, 2014
by David Chapman
Paperback
$10⁰⁰ ✓prime

Other Formats: Kindle Edition

The Believer's Deliverance Handbook: 7 Levels of Demonic Involvement and How to Minister Deliverance
Jan 29, 2014
by David Chapman
Paperback
$7⁰⁰ ✓prime

Other Formats: Kindle Edition

Caught Up: The Rapture of the Church Jun 24, 2015
by David Chapman
Paperback
$10⁰⁰ ✓prime

Other Formats: Kindle Edition

Modern Day Apostles: The Supernatural Ministry of the Apostle in the Modern Day Church Mar 4, 2014
by David Chapman
Paperback
$10⁰⁰ ✓prime

Other Formats: Kindle Edition

The Kingdom Within Aug 17, 2016
by David Chapman
Paperback
$9⁷⁸ ~~$12.00~~ ✓prime

Other Formats: Kindle Edition

Knowing God's Will: & Walking in His Blessing Nov 15, 2014
by David Chapman
Paperback
$10⁰⁰ ✓prime

Other Formats: Kindle Edition , Mass Market Paperback

The Power of the Anointing Dec 7, 2014
by David Chapman
Paperback
$10⁰⁰ ✓prime

Other Formats: Kindle Edition

Overcoming Life's Enemies Sep 10, 2016
by David Chapman
Paperback
$10⁰⁰ ✓prime

Other Formats: Kindle Edition

Unlocking the Power of Honor Aug 9, 2018
by David Chapman
Paperback
$10⁰⁰ ✓prime

Counted Faithful: Verse-by-Verse Commentary on I Timothy Jun 1, 2017
by Dr. David Chapman
Paperback
$12⁰⁰ ✓prime

Other Formats: Kindle Edition

The Pattern & The Glory: The New Testament Pattern for the Glorious End-Time Church Jul 30, 2015
by David Chapman
Paperback
$12.00 ✓prime

Other Formats: Kindle Edition

Thus Saith The Lord: Prophecy & Tongues May 15, 2014
by David Chapman
Paperback
$8.00 ✓prime

Other Formats: Kindle Edition

The Seven Letters of Jesus: God's Message to the End-Time Church Nov 16, 2015
by David A Chapman
Paperback
$10.00 ✓prime

Other Formats: Kindle Edition

The Fullness of the Spirit: How to be Filled with the Holy Spirit & Walk in Victory Feb 26, 2014
by David A Chapman
Paperback
$10.00 ✓prime

Other Formats: Kindle Edition

Blood Covenant: The Power of the Blood of Jesus Feb 3, 2014
by David Chapman
Paperback
$10.00 ✓prime

Other Formats: Kindle Edition

The Fruitful Life Mar 3, 2020
by David Chapman
Paperback
$10.00
Usually ships within 3 days.
More Buying Choices
$10.00 (6 Used & New offers)

You may contact David Chapman by writing to:

TRU Publishing
Attn: David Chapman
1726 S. 1st Ave.
Safford, Arizona 85546

Or by emailing:
TheRiverAZ@gmail.com

www.ingramcontent.com/pod-product-compliance
Lightning Source LLC
Chambersburg PA
CBHW032004060426
42449CB00031B/403